CONNECTING WITH YOUR ANGELS KIT

GUIDEBOOK

DOREEN VIRTUE, Ph.D.

HAY HOUSE, INC.
Carlsbad, California
London • Sydney • Johannesburg
Vancouver • Hong Kong

Copyright © 2004 by Doreen Virtue

Published and distributed in the United States by: Hay House, Inc., P.O. Box 5100, Carlsbad, CA 92018-5100 • *Phone:* (760) 431-7695 or (800) 654-5126 • *Fax:* (760) 431-6948 or (800) 650-5115 • www.hayhouse.com • ***Published and distributed in Australia by:*** Hay House Australia Pty. Ltd., 18/36 Ralph St., Alexandria NSW 2015 • *Phone:* 612-9669-4299 • *Fax:* 612-9669-4144 • www.hayhouse.com.au • ***Published and distributed in the United Kingdom by:*** Hay House UK, Ltd. • Unit 62, Canalot Studios • 222 Kensal Rd., London W10 5BN • *Phone:* 44-20-8962-1230 • *Fax:* 44-20-8962-1239 • www.hayhouse.co.uk • ***Published and distributed in the Republic of South Africa by:*** Hay House SA (Pty), Ltd., P.O. Box 990, Witkoppen 2068 • *Phone/Fax:* 2711-7012233 • orders@psdprom.co.za • ***Distributed in Canada by:*** Raincoast • 9050 Shaughnessy St., Vancouver, B.C. V6P 6E5 • *Phone:* (604) 323-7100 • *Fax:* (604) 323-2600

Editorial supervision: Jill Kramer
Design: Amy Rose Szalkiewicz

All rights reserved. No part of this guidebook may be reproduced by any mechanical, photographic, or electronic process, or in the form of a phonographic recording; nor may it be stored in a retrieval system, transmitted, or otherwise be copied for public or private use—other than for "fair use" as brief quotations embodied in articles and reviews without prior written permission of the publisher. The intent of the author is only to offer information of a general nature to help you in your quest for emotional and spiritual well-being. In the event you use any of the information in this book for yourself, which is your constitutional right, the author and the publisher assume no responsibility for your actions.

Printed in China by Palace Press International

CONTENTS

Chapter 1: Introduction 5 5
Chapter 2: Who's Who in the Spirit World 9
Chapter 3: Overcoming Fears and Doubts . . . 21
Chapter 4: The Four "Clairs" 31
Chapter 5: The Angel Kit Components 43
Chapter 6: How to Connect and
Communicate with Your Angels . . 53

Chapter 7: The Angel Oracle Cards 63
- *Ask Your Angels* 65
- *Family* 67
- *Golden Opportunity* 69
- *Gratitude* 71
- *No Worries* 73
- *On the Right Path* 76
- *Romance Angels* 78
- *Self-Appreciation* 80
- *Success!* 82
- *Trust Your Intuition* 84
- *Welcome the New* 86
- *You Are Supported* 88

Artwork Ordering Information 91
About the Author 95

CHAPTER 1

Introduction

You have guardian angels who wish to convey guidance to you in practical and esoteric ways. As you read these words, your celestial companions sit right beside you. Perhaps you can feel or sense them. Using this *Connecting with Your Angels Kit,* you'll learn how to clearly hear and understand your angels' messages. You'll also discover who your angels and guides are.

I highly recommend that you read this entire guidebook before embarking on your first angel-communication session (with the help of this kit). In this booklet, you'll read the same instructions and guidance I give to my psychic-development students.

Who Are Your Angels?

Your angels are nondenominational, meaning that they're not connected with any particular organized religion. They're also nonjudgmental, which means that they don't criticize you for your perceived mistakes.

Angels protect, guide, and heal you so that you're able to fulfill God's plan of peace one person at a time (beginning with yourself). Everyone has at least two guardian angels. One is loud and bold, to ensure that you'll work on your Divine life purpose; the other is quieter, and serves to comfort and soothe you.

The word *angel* means "messenger of God." The angels bring messages from the Creator to the created, acting like Divine postal carriers. They're beautiful, light-filled, trustworthy, and powerful. You needn't worry about being "tricked" by a lower spirit, as the angels' characteristics of love and light are instantly recognizable by all who encounter them. Love and light can't be faked, because they're gifts that come directly from God. And like any gifts, the giver expects the recipients to enjoy them. In other words, you have nothing to worry about when you connect with your angels.

Speaking as a clairvoyant, I've *never* seen a person who didn't have angels with them. Yet, not everyone clearly hears their angels, and even fewer people follow their Divine messages. You can block out the voice of the Divine through lifestyle (such as abusing intoxicants), fear (worrying about making life changes), or low self-esteem (not believing that you deserve good).

Your angels know that you (like all of us) have a very important life mission, which only you can fulfill. Like a player in an orchestra, your music is needed for the total harmony of the world. And while it's true that you can spiritually grow through pain, it's also true that you can grow faster through peace. You also inspire others through your peaceful example.

So, the angels are happy to help you with whatever small or large favors that bring you and the world peace. You can't overwork or bother your angels. Because they're nonphysical and multidimensional, angels have no time or space restrictions. Please don't worry that you're pulling your angels away from more pressing matters. There's nothing more important to your angels than helping you, in whatever way that will bring you peace.

CHAPTER 2

Who's Who in the Spirit World

The spirit world, where angels live, isn't a faraway place. Heaven is all around us, in a different dimension. This is similar to the frequency bands of different radio stations all existing simultaneously.

Angels

Your angels are celestial beings who have not lived on the earth before as humans, unless they were incarnated angels previously. Incarnated angels manifest into human form either temporarily to avert a crisis, or for an entire lifetime so that they can more directly help and guide people.

You can call additional celestial angels to your side, since there are countless angels. To do so, you can either mentally or verbally ask God to send them to you, directly ask the angels to come to you, or visualize more angels with you. Any method works, as long as you ask. As stated earlier, don't worry that you're bothering the angels with your requests. They're unlimited beings who are glad to help bring you peace.

Like people, angels have specialties. You can ask for the best angels to help with a particular situation, or call upon the following specialty angels:

- **Angels of Abundance.** They guide you to make wise financial decisions, give career boosts, bring about financial windfalls, help you meet your basic needs, leave coins for you to find, and help with Divine timing in career moves.

- **Beauty Angels.** These angels help you choose the best outfit, hairstyle, and accessories for any situation; guide you to wonderful hairdressers; assist you in plucking stubborn chin hairs; bring you gifts; make you glow from the inside; and show you how very attractive you are!

- **Driving and Parking Angels.** These powerful angels help you find your destination, arrive on time, and find a parking space. (Mentally ask for a parking space before you arrive at your destination to allow the angels time to arrange a great opening for you.)

- **Family Angels.** These loving angels help you with all aspects of child rearing, including adoption and conception; assist with family projects and decisions; maintain family unity and peace; encourage family members to be open-minded and compassionate toward one another; and protect the family home.

- **Fitness Angels.** Fitness angels boost your motivation to get and keep your body physically fit, guide you to the right form of exercise, reduce or eliminate cravings; help you choose healthful foods and beverages, and keep you from feeling deprived or from making excuses.

- **Healing Angels.** They surround ailing persons with healing energy; calm worries about health; guide your decisions about health care; help aspiring or current healers; and release negativity, such as anger or pessimism.

- **Moving Angels.** These angels guide you to find the perfect new home, help you sell or rent your previous home, assist with financing and qualifying for a new residence, ease

- **Nature Angels.** Also known as devas, fairies, and elementals, these special angels are guardians to plants, bodies of water, and domestic and wild animals. They assist you with gardening, or attracting birds and butterflies to your garden; guide you to make ecologically sound choices; urge you to pick up trash during outdoor walks; and help those who wish to adopt a vegetarian or vegan lifestyle.

- **Romance Angels.** These cherubic angels bring people together, heal troublesome relationships (and add fun and passion to them), and offer guidance about readying yourself to meet your soul mate. the moving process, keep moving-related stress to a minimum, and protect your belongings during the move.

- **Warrior Angels.** These angels peacefully and lovingly fight on behalf of underdogs and social issues, help grassroots causes; assist charitable organizations, protect children and guard against domestic violence, safeguard your home and valuables, give courage and outlets to those who wish to speak or write about injustices, and help pro bono lawyers.

Archangels

Archangels are the managers of the angels. They are one type of the nine varieties of angels (which include angels, archangels, principalities, powers, virtues, dominions, thrones, cherubim, and seraphim). Of these forms of angels, the angels and archangels are the most involved with helping Earth and her inhabitants.

Archangels are larger and more powerful than angels. They're nonphysical, yet they're very perceptible, audible, and visible as you tune in to them. As nonphysical celestial beings, they don't have genders. However, their specific fortes and characteristics give them distinctive male and female energies and personas.

Studies and writings about archangels reflect ancient, nondenominational viewpoints. Old monotheistic spiritual texts list 15 archangels. They're sometimes called by different names, but here are their most common ones, along with their specialties and characteristics:

- *Ariel:* Her name means "Lioness of God." She heals and helps wild animals and the environment.

- *Azrael:* His name means "Whom God Helps." He heals the grief-stricken, and also helps those who are consoling the bereaved.

- *Chamuel:* His name means "He Who Sees God." He eases anxiety; brings about global and personal peace; and helps to find lost objects, situations, and people.

- *Gabriel:* Her name means "Messenger of God." She heals women during pregnancy and childbirth, and relieves anxiety regarding creative projects. She particularly assists parents, journalists, and orators.

- *Haniel:* Her name means "Glory of God." She supports women during their monthly cycles and helps with clairvoyance.

- *Jeremiel:* His name means "Mercy of God." He deals with emotions, helping us review and take inventory of our lives so that we may forgive, and plan for positive change.

- *Jophiel:* Her name means "Beauty of God." She heals negative and chaotic situations; and brings beauty and organization to our thoughts, home, office, and other environments.

- *Metatron:* He was the prophet Enoch. He heals learning disorders and childhood issues, and helps with the new Indigo and Crystal Children.

- *Michael:* His name means "He Who Is Like God." He releases us from fear and doubt, protects us, and clears away negativity.

- *Raguel:* His name means "Friend of God." He brings harmony to all relationships, and helps to heal misunderstandings.

- *Raphael:* His name means "He Who Heals." He heals human and animal physical ailments and guides healers and would-be healers.

- *Raziel:* His name means "Secrets of God." He heals spiritual and psychic blocks, and helps us with dream interpretations and past-life memories.

- *Sandalphon:* He was the prophet Elijah. He heals aggressive tendencies, and helps musicians and music used for healing purposes.

- *Uriel:* His name means "God Is Light." He heals resentment and unforgiveness, and gives us insight and new ideas.

- *Zadkiel:* His name means "Righteousness of God." He heals memory problems and assists with other mental functions.

Ascended Masters

Great spiritual teachers and healers who help us from the spirit world are called *ascended masters.* They include Jesus, Moses, Kuan Yin, and deities from all world religions and cultures. Ascended masters help anyone who calls upon them, regardless of that person's religious affiliation. By using the methods discussed in this kit, you can learn to receive a great deal of guidance from them.

Deceased Loved Ones

Your deceased loved ones also exist in the spirit world, but they function at an energy frequency that's different from your angels. We refer to deceased loved ones as *spirit guides* to distinguish them from angels. Although they can act as angels, deceased loved ones still have human egos, which means that their guidance isn't as pure as the angels'.

You can definitely use this kit to contact your deceased loved ones. I recommend doing so if you have unfinished business with them, such as unresolved feelings of anger, or if you worry about their degree of happiness. You can certainly get advice from a deceased loved one; however, take it with the same healthy skepticism you'd employ when being advised by a living person.

Remember: People don't become saints or psychics just because they've passed on. They may have more patience and more insight from the perspective of the spirit plane, but they're still Uncle Fred and Aunt Harriet, meaning that they retain their earthly personalities and quirks. And while they're happy to help you, especially when it comes to topics related to their earthly specialty (for example, if Uncle Fred was a banker, he'll gladly give you financial guidance), it's best to consult the Creator and the angels for trustworthy advice about the major issues in life.

You can also get in touch with departed loved ones who didn't have the ability to speak your language at the time of their death. In other words, unborn children, babies, and those who were mute or otherwise unable to communicate can converse with you in the universal language of feelings, visions, or in other nonverbal ways.

Don't worry that you're bothering your deceased loved ones if you contact them. People in the spirit world, like those on Earth, have free will. If they're busy, they'll send a message through the ethers or through another departed loved one. Truly, the only thing that holds back deceased loved ones is any unhealed grief you feel toward them. Departed loved ones welcome the opportunity to deliver the healing message that they love you and are doing well in the afterlife plane.

It's normal to grieve heavily for about six months following a loss, but then gradually the depression and anger wear away. However, some grieving people put their lives on hold for years following a loss. I've met people who were suicidal, addicted to sleeping pills, or housebound due to their unrelenting grief. This behavior can block departed loved ones from their spiritual growth. The greatest favor you can do for someone who has passed away is to heal your heart of grief. Ways to do that include joining a support group, connecting with your departed loved one to reassure yourself that all is well, journaling, and taking excellent care of your body

Departed Pets

Your deceased pet can also function as a spirit guide, so far as you may feel, sense, or see its spiritual presence. The soul of the animal lives on, and stays with you as if your mutual love is a leash connecting you both. This kit can definitely assist you if you wish to connect with a departed pet.

Power Animals

A power animal is an animal spirit guide who represents that animal species, as opposed to an animal you were personally acquainted with during its lifetime. Many cultures recognize the presence of power animals as spiritual helpers. Usually, these are exotic wild animals such as bears, lions, and owls. (If you'd like more information on this subject, please read Steven D. Farmer's book *Power Animals,* which is published by Hay House.)

Other Spirit Guides

Some people have human spirit guides who aren't deceased loved ones from this lifetime—instead, these spirit guides are assigned to help with specific skills. Often, these guides are ethnic healers and exotic sages, such as Native American medicine men or women or Asian mystics.

CHAPTER 3

Overcoming Fears and Doubts

Since you (like everyone) have guardian angels, and because scientific studies show that intuition is an inherent human characteristic, you *can* have clear conversations with your angels. The first step is to address any fears so that they don't block your Divine communications.

In my experience teaching angel-communication classes worldwide since 1996 to thousands of people of all ages and backgrounds, I've found that fear is the main factor that blocks us. Instead of ignoring the fears, though, it's best to acknowledge and confront them. That way, they won't have power over you.

Here are the most common fears (posed in the form of questions) that people face when they decide to speak to their angels. As you read the information below, notice if it triggers any bodily reactions within you, or any recognition of "This sounds like me!" Give any fears that you recognize to Heaven by imagining that each fear is surrounded by a ball of light, which you pass to the angels that circle you now. Feel the release as you hand over these fears. We'll work with other fear-releasing methods later.

1. "Is it blasphemous to talk to angels?" This fear stems from some organized religions' interpretation of spiritual texts. If you truly believe that you should only speak with God, Jesus, or some other spiritual being, then don't violate that belief. To do so would cause unnecessary fear, and we certainly don't want to add to that negative emotion.

However, do consider this: The word *angel,* as stated earlier, means "Messenger of God." Angels are gifts from the Creator who act like heavenly postal carriers, bringing messages to and from the Creator and the Created. They operate with Divine precision in delivering trustworthy guidance to us. And just like any gift, the giver (the Creator) wishes us to enjoy and use the gift. The Bible and other spiritual texts are filled with positive accounts of people talking to angels, and this natural phenomenon carries into the present day.

2. "What if I don't receive a message?" The number one reason why people become blocked with respect to angelic communication is that they try too hard to make something happen. Usually, that strain comes from the underlying fear that they won't be able to hear their angels, or that maybe they don't *have* any guardian angels.

When contacting your angels, your experience will be influenced by your underlying beliefs. Holding fear-based thoughts will block you from clearly hearing your angels. However, maintaining an optimistic outlook will sharply enhance your angelic connections. The bottom line is: Don't push, strain, or try to force anything to happen. Let God and the angels do all the work when sending you Divine messages. Your job is simply to be receptive, and to notice all of the impressions (thoughts, feelings, visions, or words) that come to you.

3. "What if I'm wrong, or just making it up?" True Divine guidance is uplifting, inspiring, motivational, positive, and loving. Angel messages always mention how to improve something: an outlook, one's health, relationships, the environment, the world, and so on. Angels generally repeat the message through your feelings, thoughts, visions, and hearing until you take the advised action. If you're unsure if a message is real or not, wait awhile, as true Divine guidance repeats itself, while false guidance eventually fades away if ignored.

Watch out for the very common "Impostor Phenomenon," in which the ego tries to convince you that you're not qualified to talk to angels and that you don't have intuitive or psychic abilities. Know that this message is fear- and ego-based.

4. "Isn't it better for me to learn life's lessons on my own?" Some people feel that they're "cheating" by requesting Divine intervention. They believe that we're supposed to suffer in order to learn and grow, and that we're responsible for getting ourselves in and out of jams. Yet the angels say that while we can grow through suffering, we can grow even faster through peace. And our peacefulness inspires others in ways that suffering cannot.

The angels won't do everything for you, though. They're more like teammates who ask you to pass the ball as you collectively move toward each goal. As you ask them for help, the angels will sometimes create a miraculous intervention. But more often, they'll help you by delivering Divine guidance so that you can help yourself.

5. "How can I be certain that I'm really speaking to an angel?" God, the archangels, ascended masters, and angels all speak in loving and positive words. They use phrasing such as *you* and *we,* as would anyone who was talking to you (while the ego will use the word *I* at the beginning of sentences). Your departed loved ones will use phrases, words, and mannerisms that are similar to those they employed when they were living.

If you ever hear negative words from anyone, living or passed, stop talking to them and immediately pray for the assistance of Archangel Michael. He'll escort lower energies away and protect you from negativity.

Talking with angels is a pleasant, uplifting experience. Whether you hear them, see them, feel their presence, or receive new insights, you'll certainly enjoy connecting with them.

Handling and Healing Ego-Based Fears

Occasionally, you may doubt the validity of your angelic communications. When this occurs, the angels can help buoy your faith in your spiritual-communication abilities. Here are some tried-and-true methods for handling and healing these fears and insecurities:

Ask for a Sign. Even though you may be unsure about whether or not you're hearing your angels, rest assured that they hear *you*. So when you doubt yourself, ask your angels to give you a sign verifying the validity of their messages. You can convey this request mentally, verbally, or by writing it in a letter. Don't tell the angels how you want your sign to appear—just ask them to give you a clear sign that you can easily recognize, to assure you that you've correctly heard their messages.

Then, be extra alert for unusual happenings related to the topic of your angelic communications. For instance, if you asked your angels about a particular person, you may hear songs that you associate with that individual, or you might meet people with the same name.

Generally, if you hear, see, think, or feel a message three times or more, it's a sign.

Ask for Help. Conversational skills are no different with angels than with living people, in that you must make your needs clearly known. For example, if someone were to speak to you in an inaudible whisper, you'd ask that person to speak up. Or if someone wasn't making sense or was using cryptic language, you'd ask that person to clarify their meaning. Don't be afraid to do the same with your angels.

If you can't hear the angels, ask them to speak louder. If you don't understand their messages, ask them for additional details.

Make Sure You Really Want to Communicate. If you're afraid to communicate with an angel or deceased loved one, then you won't allow it to happen. And Heaven doesn't want to frighten you by forcing their messages upon you. Have an honest talk with yourself and your angels to make sure that you truly wish to see and hear them.

Turn It Over. Don't carry your doubts single-handedly! Instead, give them to your angels. To do this, you can inhale deeply, and imagine blowing your fears to your guardian angels on the exhale. Or, envision handing a bubble of fear to the angels. They'll take the fears to the Divine light for transmutation, and leave only the lessons and the love. You can also write a letter to your guardian angels about any concerns, and ask for their assistance.

Remember: It's not whether you have fears, it's how you handle them that counts.

Call Upon Jophiel. As described in Chapter 2, Archangel Jophiel's name means "Beauty of God." One of her roles is to beautify your thoughts so that they're steered away from worry and pessimism, and toward faith and optimism. When you notice your thoughts spiraling into "Ain't it awful" patterns, call upon Jophiel to boost your point of view. Simply think, *Jophiel, please help!* and she'll immediately come to your assistance. Please note, however, that if you work with Jophiel, she'll also urge you to beautify your living and work spaces as well. So don't be surprised if you suddenly become motivated to organize your closets!

Easy Does It. Be sure that your shoulders are relaxed and that you're breathing deeply while contacting your angels. A relaxed mind and body are the gateway to your psychic higher self. Straining, pushing, or trying to hear the angels puts you into the "unpsychic" lower self of the ego.

If you get uptight during an angel reading, take a moment to center yourself: Close your eyes, let go of time worries, and take three very deep breaths. Picture a beam of white light coming through the top of your head and into your body, magnetizing any stressful energy. Mentally call upon your angels to assist you, and then begin or resume your angel reading.

Check Your Lifestyle. One reason why angels commonly urge us to improve our diet, sleep patterns, and exercise habits is because lifestyle affects psychic and intuitive awareness. A heavy, chemical-laden diet, along with poor sleep and exercise routines, cloud thinking abilities and lower energy levels. Eat, sleep, and exercise for optimal mental alertness, and you'll find that your angelic transmissions greatly improve. Typically, this means eating a predominantly vegetarian diet, drinking lots of water, avoiding chemicals, setting aside sufficient sleeping time, and exercising regularly. Your angels will give you details about the best lifestyle for you if you ask for their guidance. And when angels ask you to change the way you're living, their repetitive advice is difficult to ignore!

Practice, Practice, Practice. Ultimately, as with any skill, practice helps us develop confidence in our abilities to communicate with Heaven, so don't get discouraged if your first few attempts don't yield immediate success. Instead, take an adventurous attitude toward working in harmonious partnership with your angels.

Keep notes in your journal related to your angel-communication sessions. You'll soon notice the accuracy with which your angels predict your future, and guide you in making life-affirming choices. You'll also notice important patterns among your angel messages, which can be a form of Divine guidance in themselves.

CHAPTER 4

The Four "Clairs"

Since you have guardian angels with you continuously, you receive angelic messages every day. The question isn't *whether* your angels talk to you, but whether you *notice* their communications. That's because angels may speak to you in ways that differ from your expectations.

Angels, along with other heavenly beings, communicate in four ways:

1. Through Visions: This applies to things that you see mentally or with your physical eyes, what you see in dreams, signs that appear before you, seeing flashing or sparkling lights, sensing light orbs in photographs, seeing moving objects, or noticing number sequences repeatedly such as 444 or 111. This is called *clairvoyance,* which means "clear seeing."

2. Through Feelings: These are emotions that come out of the blue, such as joy, excitement, and compassion; physical feelings disconnected to the physical world, such as feeling suddenly warm or feeling changes in air temperature or air pressure; sensing a spiritual presence; feeling as if someone has touched you; or smelling an essence with no physical origin, such as flowers or smoke. This is called *clairsentience,* which means "clear feeling."

3. Through Sounds: This refers to hearing your name called as you awaken, celestial-sounding music from out of nowhere, a warning from a disembodied voice, overhearing a conversation or radio/TV program that gives you the exact information you need, a loving message in your mind or outside one ear, or a high-pitched ringing sound. This is called *clairaudience,* which means "clear hearing."

4. Through Thoughts: This is when you know something without knowing *how* you know; receiving an "aha!" revelation; being able to fix an item without instructions; having very wise words come through your speech or writings, as if someone else gave them to you; getting a great idea for a new invention, business, or product; and experiencing "I knew that!" thoughts after something occurs. This is called *claircognizance,* which means "clear thinking."

What's Your "Primary Clair"?

While the angels talk to us in a combination of four ways—visions, feelings, sounds, and thoughts—one of these channels is strongest for you. We call this your "primary clair." Like the first cylinder to fire up in a four-cylinder automobile engine, this is the basic way that your incoming angelic messages are received. The other three clairs amplify and augment this primary means of angelic communication.

You've probably heard that some people are highly visual, while others are more auditory or kinesthetic, and so on. These individual styles reflect how you notice the material world with your physical senses, as well as how you receive and notice Divine communication.

To discover your primary clair, think about the following scenarios, and then answer the question (choose only one response for each question).

1. **When you initially meet someone new, what's the first thing you tend to notice about the person?**

    a. The way that the person looks, such as clothing, hair, teeth, shoes, or general attractiveness.

   b. How you feel around the person, such as being comfortable, amused, safe, and so on.

   c. Whether you find the person interesting, or believe this may be someone who can help you out in your career.

   d. The sound of the person's voice or laughter.

2. Think back on a vacation you took. What stands out most in your memory?

   a. The beautiful sights of nature, architecture, or something that you witnessed.

   b. The peaceful, romantic, restful, exhilarating feelings associated with the trip.

   c. The important and interesting cultural and/or historical information (or skills) that you learned while traveling.

   d. The sweet silence, the crashing surf, the chirping birds, the rustling leaves, music, or some other sound.

3. **Recall a movie that you truly enjoyed. When you think of that film, what comes to mind first?**

   a. The attractive actors and actresses, the lighting, the costumes, or the scenery.

   b. The way the movie made you laugh, cry, or moved you in some other way.

   c. The interesting story, or the life lessons that you or the movie's characters learned during the story.

   d. The musical score, or the sound of the actors' and actresses' voices.

Note your answers to the above questions. Most likely, you've answered two or three questions with the same letter. That letter signifies your primary clair, or the dominant way in which you process information about the physical and spiritual world.

This is what the answers mean:

Mostly "a" answers signify clairvoyance. You're a highly visual person and are likely to notice how people, places, and even meals look before you notice other aspects. You're probably very artistic, or if you're not creative in this way, you have an excellent eye for putting together wardrobes, interior design, and such. Visual harmony is important to you, and you appreciate anything that's pleasing to the eye. You probably see sparkling or flashing lights when angels move around you, and you've most likely seen a departed loved one out of the corner of your eye before. You have mental visions of possibilities, and you have the ability to put these intentions into action.

Your angels speak to you through mental visions; signs that you witness with your physical eyes (anything that's meaningful that you see); repeating number sequences (such as 111, 444, and so on); finding coins; seeing butterflies, birds, and colors around people; and other visual means. Trust these visions—they're Heaven's way of speaking to you!

Mostly "b" answers signify clairsentience. You interact with the world through your physical and emotional feelings. You're highly sensitive and may have difficulty dealing with crowds, which can include driving on busy streets and freeways. You sometimes confuse others' feelings for your own. You're very compassionate, and often feel the pain of others (sometimes unknowingly). You may overeat or indulge in other addictions to deal with overwhelming feelings. You want to help others to feel happy, and may become a professional helper or form relationships with people who need assistance. You've been teased for being "too sensitive," yet your sensitivity has made you a delicate receiving instrument for Heaven's messages.

Your angels speak to you through your heart and body. You feel joy as an indicator that you're on the right path; dread as a sign that changes and healing are necessary; and fatigue as a clue that you need to take time for rest, play, and self-care. You can tell whether a person is trustworthy or not, your gut feelings are accurate, you feel air-pressure and temperature changes when communicating with the spirit world, can sense the presence of angels or departed loved ones, and sometimes feel angels brushing your skin or hair. Don't write these sensations off as being "just feelings"—they're how Heaven speaks to you!

Mostly "c" answers signify claircognizance. You're an intellectual who receives direct communication through ideas and revelations. You often know facts (both trivial and important) without having read or heard anything about a particular subject before, as if God has downloaded the information directly into your brain. You're not comfortable with small talk, and prefer deeper and more profound discussions. You may feel uneasy around people, except in one-on-one situations involving a subject of interest to you. You're able to fix electronic and mechanical items without referring to instruction booklets; and you know how to heal people and situations, too. You've most likely been teased for being a "know-it-all." You may be skeptical about angels and psychic abilities, unless you've had a dramatic lifesaving experience that you can't explain away.

Your angels speak to you through wordless impressions that you receive in your mind. You're able to mentally ask for information or help and receive it as Divine instructions that suddenly appear in your thoughts. You receive brilliant ideas for inventions, teachings, and businesses that shouldn't be ignored. The "aha" moments are clues to when you're connecting with your angels. As a claircognizant, you tend to assume that your knowledge is common information. It isn't—it's Heaven's way of answering your prayers and speaking to you!

Mostly "d" answers signify clairaudience. You're very sensitive to noise, and you're the first one to cringe at off-key notes or other unpleasant sounds. You can remember song melodies in much the same way that someone with a photographic memory can remember material they've read. It's best if you use earplugs when traveling, as sensitivity to noise makes it difficult for you to sleep or relax on airplanes and in hotel rooms. For the same reason, you avoid the first few rows at loud concerts. When you use alarm clocks, you prefer waking to soft music on the radio rather than loud buzzing sounds.

Your angels speak to you with words that you hear inside or outside your mind. During emergencies, you hear a loud voice outside of one ear, which warns you of danger. The voice of Heaven, unlike an auditory hallucination, is always loving, to the point, and inspiring—even when it asks you to do something heroic, or function beyond what you believe are your capacities. You're likely to hear celestial music and your name being called in the morning. Don't worry that you're making it up, even if it sounds like your own voice. As long as the voice is loving and asks you to improve a situation, it's Heaven's way of speaking directly to you!

Clearing Your Clairs

Surveys that I've conducted throughout the world have shown that most people receive angel messages through their feelings. The second most common way to communicate with angels is through visions. Fewer people tend to get angel messages primarily through their thoughts or by actually hearing words.

You can open your primary clair, as well as the other three, to a greater degree. Some methods for doing so include stating affirmations such as, "I am profoundly clairvoyant," "I easily hear accurate and specific messages from the spirit world," "I clearly understand my angels' messages," and so forth. Avoid using negative affirmations such as "I'm just not visual" or "I never receive any messages," as these can prevent you from further opening your psychic senses. The rule of thumb is to affirm what you desire, instead of what you fear.

Another way to open your clairs is through *chakra clearing.* This involves sending Divine light to the energy centers (called *chakras,* which means "wheels" in the ancient Eastern language known as Sanskrit) in your body that regulate your psychic abilities. The chakras that correlate to each of the clairs are:

Clairvoyance:	Third-eye chakra (between the two physical eyes)
Clairsentience:	Heart chakra (in the chest)
Claircognizance:	Crown chakra (at the top of the head)
Clairaudience:	Ear chakras (above each eyebrow)

For a full explanation of chakras and ways to clear and balance them, please see my book *Chakra Clearing* (now available from Hay House in hardcover with an accompanying CD).

In addition, the time-tested spiritual practice of working with crystals also opens the chakras. Wear or hold the following crystals to open each of the clairs (the crystals can be used alone or in combination with each other):

Clairvoyance:	Amethyst; clear quartz; moonstone
Clairsentience:	Pink tourmaline; rose quartz; smithsonite
Claircognizance:	Sugilite
Clairaudience:	Phantom quartz

Now it's time to put all this information together, with help from the tools in this kit. The next chapter discusses how to prepare your kit for your angelic-communication sessions.

CHAPTER 5

The Angel Kit Components

The products in this angel kit are the same ones that I recommend to my psychic-development students. More than feel-good spa products, these are powerful tools to help you connect with your angels. So let's begin with an overview of the tools in this kit.

Dead Sea Bath Salts: The bath salts in your kit are from the Dead Sea, and they contain no artificial coloring or fragrances. The Dead Sea is located adjacent to Qumran, Israel, a home base for the ancient mystical Jewish group known as the Essenes (pronounced *ESS-eens*). The Essenes are renowned for their spiritual healing and manifestation knowledge. Many scholars believe that much of this group's wisdom is found in the books known as the Dead Sea Scrolls, which numerous experts consider to be the lost books of the Bible. Some modern mystics believe that Jesus spent his youth studying with the Essenes.

In addition, the physical makeup of Qumran makes the Dead Sea and its salt extremely therapeutic.

Qumran is located approximately 400 meters below sea level, making it the lowest land point on the planet. This creates high barometric pressure, which, combined with the Israeli heat, makes the Dead Sea water evaporate rapidly, concentrating the salt and its mineral components.

The Dead Sea is about ten times saltier than the ocean, and its salt contains 21 minerals. It also has 15 times more magnesium and 50 times more bromine than ocean water. Magnesium and bromine are both relaxing agents, so soaking in a bath filled with Dead Sea salt promotes relaxation.

It's therapeutic to soak regularly in warm salt water, preferably in Dead Sea salts. You can purchase more at most health-food stores or online from various sources (just type the keywords "Dead Sea salt" into an internet search engine). Be sure that your bath salts are all-natural, without artificial ingredients.

Soaking in warm sea salt helps you release psychic and physical toxins. It clears your heart chakra, and relaxes your mind and body. Salt draws toxins out of your pores, because the water breaks the salt's molecules apart (NaCl separates into Na and Cl). This conducts the salt's electrons faster, which energetically clears and massages you. The warmer and saltier your bath, the greater this effect.

The high mineral content of Dead Sea salts also softens your skin. You can add to the experience by pouring pure essential oils (available at health-food stores) into your bathwater. Try lavender oil to promote relaxation and sleep, and a small amount of eucalyptus (too much could possibly burn your skin, so use caution) to awaken and energize you. You can also pour dried herbs into the water, such as sage for clearing negative energy. In addition, try sprinkling dried or fresh flower petals such as rose or lavender into the bath to add beauty and fragrance.

A Rose Quartz Crystal: Crystals come from deep within the earth, and possess amazing healing properties and great beauty. Archaeologists and mystics have found evidence of crystals being used in healings and spiritual ceremonies since ancient times. Crystals amplify natural energy in a process called *piezoelectricity*. Today, hospitals use quartz crystals, microbalancers, and piezoelectric crystal sensors in diagnostic and healing work. And crystals are routinely used in radios, watches, and other electronic devices.

Crystals can boost the light and energy of our chakra system and our energy body, and they can heal imbalances as well. I personally use them to amplify the energy of my angel readings, and find that—in the same way they're used to conduct energy in radios—crystals boost the volume and details I receive during my psychic-reading sessions.

Each type of crystal has a specific function. The heart-shaped crystal in your kit is known as "rose quartz," since it has a rose-pink coloring and comes from the quartz family of crystals. Quartz is available in clear (and many other colors, too). The color of the quartz, or any other form of crystal, partly determines which healing purpose it serves.

Rose quartz is widely regarded as the "heart-chakra crystal." This chakra is important when doing psychic or intuitive work because angelic messages are love based. When our hearts are closed because of fear or emotional pain, we may not recognize or receive messages of love. Opening our hearts, then, is essential to clearly hearing and receiving our angels' messages.

The heart chakra also helps us feel and interpret clairsentience. As described in the previous chapter, clairsentience means receiving intuitive messages through physical or emotional feelings, including fragrances and aromas. This is the most common way in which people receive angelic messages.

An open heart chakra is also helpful when manifesting a better love life, whether this involves attracting a soul mate, or healing an existing relationship. The heart shape of the crystal in this kit gives it additional power in opening the channels of love, intuition, and clairsentience.

Incense: The Nag Champa incense in this angel kit will help open clairvoyance, which is the ability to see angels and psychic visions. Ancient Eastern mystics teach that closely watching incense smoke tends to enhance one's clairvoyant sensitivities. Looking at and studying how the smoke bends and dances can magnify the awareness of mental visions, dreams, and seeing angels and guides.

The scent of Nag Champa is widely hailed as a relaxation tool. Its pleasant, all-natural fragrance also helps with meditation, focusing, and feeling centered. The angels say that we can better access them if we pay attention to that which is intangible, such as smells, lighting, and music. Incense is one way to bring these sensations into the home. It feels as if one is in a yoga studio or ashram when Nag Champa is burning.

You can purchase additional Nag Champa incense at metaphyical and health-food stores, or online. Incense burners, which prop up the incense stick, are also available through those venues. Or, you can place the lit incense stick into a soft piece of soap, an unlit candle, a glass filled with pebbles, or any item that props up the stick up and keeps it away from flammables.

A White Candle: Candles are another focusing tool, because you can stare at the flame and shut out mental and visual distractions. Ancient esoteric practices teach about the function of the particular color of candle used in spiritual ceremonies. White candles are commonly used to amplify and purify prayer. They're also powerful for manifestation.

Looking at the flame of a white candle while simultaneously thinking about what you want can help quickly bring it about. Your desire to communicate with your guardian angels and spirit guides can be rapidly manifested by holding that thought while staring at the candle.

12 Angel Oracle Cards: Based on ancient Pythagorean sacred numerology, oracle cards are a tool for seeing into the future. They also validate the feelings, thoughts, visions, and words you receive during a reading by confirming that you clearly communicated with your angels. In addition, the cards can help clarify and expand upon any messages you receive from Heaven.

Since some people are frightened by the images and symbology on tarot cards, angel cards were created at the urging of the angelic realm. The cards in this kit contain only loving and life-affirming messages, reflecting the communication style of the angels.

Sometimes when people are stressed, they have difficulty hearing their angels. This is because their fear makes them more aware of their worries than of the encouraging guidance of the angels. Also, stressed people often engage in shallow breathing. Deep breathing is key to increasing psychic and intuitive awareness.

There are 12 original Angel Oracle Cards in this kit. In the next two chapters, you'll read about specific ways to use these cards to discern your angels' messages.

A Journal: The journal enclosed in this kit is designed to encourage your angelic communication. Some of the pages have instructions at the top with suggested questions and topics for your angel sessions. The first few exercises in the journal correspond to the guidance on Track 2 of your angel kit's CD as well. The blank pages are for you to discuss anything you like with your angels. When you fill up this journal, please buy other blank journals (Hay House publishes several) so that you'll have ready access to this important record of your angelic conversations.

As you ask questions of your angels, you'll receive answers that you'll want to write down in your journal. You may find that the answers come through a process known as *automatic writing*. This means that the pen may seem to take on a life on its own, as if the angels are writing for you. Or, you may "hear" a voice giving you dictation. For some people, the angels present visions that you'll need to describe in your writing. And if you receive ideas or knowledge, you'll want to write that down as well.

Automatic writing is safe and pleasant, but if you ever find it frightening, mentally ask Archangel Michael to protect you and your writing. Michael ensures that only beings of Divine light surround and write through you. Michael helps you release any control issues as well. He never wants you to give up control or awareness of your actions. In fact, many people prefer to invoke Michael at the start of their automatic-writing sessions.

Angel Communication CD: The CD that's included in this kit contains a guided meditation with uplifting music, designed to help you access the angelic realm. There are four different tracks on the CD:

Track 1: *Clearing and Opening to the Angelic Realm.* This is a guided meditation to help you connect with your angels using the tools in this kit. Play this track once you're ready to conduct an angel session. It will walk you through the process of detoxing and opening yourself energetically and psychically, using the Dead Sea bath salts, the white candle, and Nag Champa incense. Relaxing and ethereal music will help you relax, focus, and tune in to the spirit world.

Track 2: *Conducting an Angel Reading for Yourself.* After you've completed your Dead Sea salt bath and have climbed out, you're ready to use the other products in the kit. Track 2 walks you through the process of conducting an angel reading for yourself using the rose quartz crystal, the oracle cards, and the journal.

Track 3: *Giving Someone Else an Angel Reading.* This track guides you along as you give angel readings to other people.

Track 4: *Meet Your Guardian Angels and Spirit Guides.* This guided meditation helps you identify who's with you as an angel or guide, and gain a closer relationship with them. This track also guides you as you ask for and receive information, answers, and guidance from guardian angels, archangels, departed loved ones, and Heaven.

You can use this CD in conjunction with the other tools in your kit, or on its own. Whether you wish to contact a departed loved one, your guardian angels, or get a message from Heaven, the CD will greatly assist you.

CHAPTER 6

How to Connect and Communicate with Your Angels

Now it's time to use the items in this kit to initiate a discussion with your angels. The first few times that you use this kit, please follow the steps outlined below. After that, your angels may guide you to add to or change some of the steps. Feel free to follow whatever guidance they give you. As long as you feel happy, comfortable, and safe, you can rest assured that you're following your angels' lead.

However, if you ever feel fearful or angry during an angel session, then stop what you're doing and pray for assistance from Archangel Michael and anyone else with whom you feel spiritually or religiously aligned. He will help to correct any situation that goes awry. However, it's rare that you'll have any negative experiences when contacting angels. Their powerful energy assures that the session will be guided and supported by Divine love.

Step 1: Prepare the Items in Your Kit. Although I've infused your kit with angelic blessings and protective energy, you'll want to clear and consecrate the kit to make it your own. You can do this anytime prior to your first angel communication session.

— *The Angel Kit.* First, pray over the entire angel kit (with the contents still in the box). Ask your guardian angels and the archangels to bless all of your sessions using the kit, and request that they clear away any negative energy that the kit may have inadvertently absorbed from the time of its manufacture until you acquired it.

— *Rose Quartz Crystal.* If it's a sunny day or a moonlit evening, place your rose quartz crystal outdoors for two to three hours. Fresh air, sunshine, and moonlight are three of the most effective means for clearing old energy from a crystal.

If the weather or your schedule doesn't permit you to put the crystal outdoors, then use this alternate method: Hold the crystal in your dominant hand (the one that you favor when you write). With your arm next to your side, hold the crystal so that it faces the ground or floor. Say silently or aloud: "I ask that Mother Earth absorb any lower energies from this crystal, and transmute them into Divine love." Wait a moment while the transfer process occurs.

Then, hold the crystal above your head so that it faces the sky or ceiling and say, "I ask that Divine love and only Divine love be infused into this crystal now." Spend a moment allowing your beautiful rose quartz crystal to be filled with powerful and loving energy.

— *Angel Oracle Cards*. Hold the pack of angel cards in your nondominant hand. Make your dominant hand into a fist, and tap the card deck with your knuckles once. This knocks out any old or negative energy. Then, touch each card briefly to infuse your personal energy fingerprint into each one. When you've touched each of the 12 cards, fan them out. Place the fanned cards on your chest, with the pictures facing you. Say this prayer through your heart, into the cards: "I ask that all of my readings be very accurate, specific, and filled with blessings. Please help me get my ego out of my way; and clearly hear, see, feel, and know the Divine messages that want to come through. Please oversee and protect all of my readings. Thank you, and Amen."

This step should be repeated once a month or so, or after anyone touches the items in the kit (other people's energy needs to be cleared from the items so that they solely belong to you and your angels).

Step 2: Create a Quiet, Sanctuary-Type Environment. Soaking in your bathtub at home is ideal for conducting your first few angel sessions. (Once you become accustomed to the sound of your angels, you'll be able to hear them more easily in noisier, more public situations). Either wait until your housemates are gone, or put a "Do Not Disturb" sign on the door. Make sure that telephones and pagers are turned off, or are out of hearing range. Ask your angels to hold your calls, and to help ensure your privacy in all ways. If possible, keep the lights in the room low to create a more relaxing atmosphere.

Step 3: Prepare Yourself. Angel sessions are best conducted when your system is relatively free of chemicals, so wait a few hours after ingesting caffeine or nicotine, for instance. It's best not to consume alcohol or other intoxicants within eight hours of an angel session, as a clear mind better picks up the angels' communications. Prepare a meal prior to your angel session that's light and healthful, preferably including fresh and organic produce. Chocolate, red meat, and heavy dairy products (such as cream or cheese) also interfere with some people's abilities to hear their angels. Pineapple, oranges, and other tropical citrus fruits seem to boost psychic skills. Your best bet is to eat a vegetable or fruit salad prior to your session.

As you prepare for your session, maintain a positive and optimistic outlook. Stay mentally connected to your angels through prayer, silently asking them for help with whatever you need. Remember: Even if you can't hear them yet, your angels definitely hear *you*. Breathe deeply, and move slowly but deliberately as you prepare for your session.

Step 4: Assemble Your Angel Kit Items. Bring your angel kit into the room with you. You'll also need the following items:

- A CD player
- Matches or a lighter
- Holders for the candle and incense
- A pen
- Drinking water to refresh yourself during the session
- A bathtub pillow (or folded towel) to comfortably lean your neck and head against once you're in the tub

First, light the incense and candle, place them into holders, and put them on a stable surface where you'll see them once you're inside the bathtub.

Next, fill the tub with water that's as warm as you can comfortably stand without scalding yourself. This allows the water to stay warm during the length of your angel session, and also activates the salt's detoxification action. Pour the bath salts into the steaming water to dissolve them, and mix them with the bathwater. Although it may sound relaxing and romantic to drink a glass of champagne in the tub, this isn't a time to cloud the mind or body with intoxicants. The point of the bath is to detoxify lower energies and impurities.

Step 5: Open Yourself Up to the Angels. Put the CD from the kit into the CD player, press play for Track 1, adjust the CD volume, and if the water temperature suits you, disrobe and climb into the bathtub. Get yourself into a comfortable position. Breathe and center yourself, and follow the guidance on the CD until Track 1 ends.

Step 6: Receiving and Recording Your Messages. At the end of Track 1, thank the candle and incense for their help as you blow them out. Gently and slowly leave the bathtub. Dry yourself; and don a towel, robe, or comfortable clothing. Get your journal, angel cards, pen, the CD and player, and the rose quartz crystal. Take them with you to a comfortable place where you can recline in private, such as on a rug or towel on the bathroom floor, a bed, or a sofa. Sit so that you're comfortable, with your upper body in a reclining position, leaning against a pillow or stationary object that's cushioned by a towel.

Play Track 2 of the CD in order to utilize your journal, crystal, and angel cards for your angelic communication.

Using the Angel Kit Without the CD

Once you've listened to the CD several times, you'll begin to incorporate the methods yourself. Soon you may feel that you don't need the CD to guide your angelic communications. The items in your kit can be used without the CD.

For instance, you can increase your clairvoyant sensitivity by staring at the smoke of the lit incense stick. As you gaze at the incense, mentally ask your angels to help you better see them and access their messages. Then stare at the lit white candle while you simultaneously imagine yourself successfully communicating with your angels. Feel the sense of happiness that comes from having regular discussions with your angels. Hold these thoughts, visions, and feelings as you stare into the white candle. Give thanks that this desire is manifesting for you right now.

Then, lie down and place the rose quartz crystal on your chest, right above your heart. Close your eyes and breathe deeply. As you inhale, think the words *I am loved.* As you exhale, breathe out any stressful thoughts or feelings. Mentally ask the angels to direct their loving energy into your heart to clear away any fears about love. The angels' energy will be boosted by the rose quartz crystal. Feel the warmth and pleasant sensations in your chest.

Sit up whenever you feel ready, and place the crystal next to you. Hold the deck of cards and think of a question, then shuffle the cards while simultaneously asking the angels that question. Your angels will signal you when to stop shuffling by sending you a feeling, thought, or word. You can't make a mistake and stop shuffling too soon. If a card "jumps" out of the pack, set it aside, faceup.

Draw three cards from the top and place them from left to right in the order they were drawn. The card to the left describes the origin of the question. The middle card gives advice about or describes the current situation related to the question. The right-hand card discusses the outcome. Any cards that jumped out during the shuffling process provide additional details about the entire reading. (The next chapter describes the deeper general meaning of each card.)

If the cards don't make immediate sense, then ask the angels to explain them to you. Take your journal and pen, and write your question at the top of a blank page. Then, close your eyes and breathe deeply while mentally asking the same question of your angels. Make sure that you're really asking the question that's important to you. The angels always address the truth, so they may be answering an underlying question that you're afraid to voice.

After you ask the question, write down the impressions that come to you. For example, notice your thoughts, words that come to mind, mental visions, physical sensations, and emotions. Write them down in your journal even if they seem to have no connection to your question. Don't worry whether you're imagining or making up the answers. If you have difficulty noticing anything in your mind or body, ask your angels to help you. It's impossible to get *nothing* from your angels because you're always thinking and feeling, so just focus on noticing your thoughts and feelings and write them down.

CHAPTER 7

The Angel Oracle Cards

This chapter provides the general meanings of the oracle cards in your kit. They're meant to be used intuitively, so look at the cards and read the words associated with them in conjunction with noticing thoughts, feelings, visions, and words. Your angels will give you additional messages, as the cards are a springboard for their communications.

The same card can have different meanings for different people, situations, and questions. *Trust* your first impression when reading the cards. (The instructions for working with them can be found in the last section of Chapter 6 and also on the accompanying CD.) You can also mix these cards with any of my other decks to get additional details and clarification.

Once you've first consulted your intuition, read the additional explanations of each oracle card on the pages that follow. You'll see that each page contains a channeled message related to the card's meaning; a list of various meanings to help you put the message into context (although this isn't an exhaustive list, and you should always trust your intuition as the final authority); and suggested actions to take to help put the angels' message into action.

ASK YOUR ANGELS

Request that your guardian angels help you,
and trust the messages you receive from them.

Message from Your Angels: "We can only help you with this situation insofar as you will invite our participation and allow us to guide and support you. Without your express invitation, our intervention is restricted to loving you unconditionally while watching at the sidelines. We humbly ask that you allow for our more direct intervention by giving us explicit permission to help and assist. Your request is immediately answered, and we shall endeavor to bring about the awareness of order and Divine love."

Various Meanings of the Card: Specifically ask your angels to help you with this situation. • Ask your "Earth Angels" such as family and friends for help. • Be open to receiving help. • The answer to your prayer will be positive, yet it will look different than you expect. • You're not alone. • Your angels want to help you now!

Suggested Actions to Take After Drawing This Card: Take a moment right now to specifically ask your angels for help, either silently or aloud. • Write a letter to your angels, requesting their assistance. • Affirm: *"It is safe for me to ask for and receive help, support, and love"* two or more times a day. • Ask a person to help you with something, and just say "Thank you" without apologizing.

FAMILY

Your family members are safe, loved,
and protected by the angels.

Message from Your Angels: "Families are earthly soul groups who choose to incarnate together for various reasons and purposes. Sometimes families become riddled with fear, and become unbalanced and unpleasant. Yet, each family is always supported by a base of Divine love that can never be shattered or exhausted. *You* are an angel within your family because of your desire to amplify this love. Focus upon the truth within your family: that angels watch over all of you, and God's love permeates every family member and situation."

Various Meanings of the Card: There will be a new addition to your family. • Your family loves you (regardless of appearances). • There will be a healing within the family. • Reach out to your family. • Something related to going home, or a change of family residence, will occur. • There will be a transition, with help and support from the angels. • Family members who've crossed over are sending you an "I love you" message. • You have a spiritual family of wonderful friends who want to help you with this situation. • Focus upon the inner Divine light of family members, instead of on their ego personalities.

Suggested Actions to Take After Drawing This Card: Spend a moment meditating about your family, and send loving prayers to any person who comes to mind. • Call or write a family member you're thinking about. • Ask a friend or family member to help you. • Have a silent conversation with a departed family member. • Ask a family member's angels to effect a healing.

GOLDEN OPPORTUNITY

Your prayers have been answered.

Message from Your Angels: "Although you may not feel entirely ready and qualified, Divine timing has brought you an opportunity to learn, grow, and excel. Change and growth can sometimes feel threatening, yet we are here to assure you that it is as natural as flowers blossoming and the sun rising. You are part of God's Great Plan of Peace, and it is important for you to honor your Divine assignments as they come to you. This new situation gives you many opportunities to make a positive difference in the world. Instead of becoming fearful, we ask you to fully embrace the opportunity; and enjoy watching yourself grow, learn, and contribute!"

Various Meanings of the Card: A new door is opening for you—walk through it without delay! • Your prayer is answered in an unexpected way. • Golden Christ energy surrounds you and this situation. • Your clairvoyance is opening. • Have patience with Divine timing, and don't try to force anything to happen. • Pay extra-careful attention to repetitive signs, such as meaningful messages that you see, hear, think, or feel.

Suggested Actions to Take After Drawing This Card: Keep a dream journal and write down the messages from your dreams each morning. • Make a list of your top priorities. • Consult with a life coach. • Affirm: *"I am perfectly qualified for each new opportunity that comes along. I always know what to do in the moment, and angels guide me every step of the way."*

GRATITUDE

Focus on what is positive in your life, and you will attract even more positive situations.

Message from Your Angels: "It is easy to slip into self-pity and pessimism when everything around you appears to be problematic, yet this is a denial of the positive, which is always present, regardless of appearances to the contrary. Find that positive under-current now by thinking about whatever you are grateful for. Your gratitude for even the simplest of gifts will have a remarkable turnaround effect, and draw more heartwarming experiences into your life.

Let gratitude elevate you out of the feeling of victimhood, and remind you that you *are* powerful and loved right now."

Various Meanings of the Card: Keep your thoughts and words focused on the positive. • As you count your blessings, you'll draw more of them into your life. • Stop complaining. • Beware of adopting a "victimhood mentality," as it will disempower you. • The Universe loves to shower gifts upon grateful people.

Suggested Actions to Take After Drawing This Card: Make a list of everything you're grateful for. • As you fall asleep and awaken, mentally count your blessings. • Meditate on the feeling of gratitude, and notice how your body feels as a result. • Practice saying "Thank you" often. • Send an "I'm grateful for you in my life" letter or e-mail to your loved ones.

No Worries

Surrender cares and worries to
God and the angels, and know that
everything is truly in Divine order.

Message from Your Angels: "We understand that your worries are your way of trying to control the situation, and to think of ways to create a better outcome. Yet, would you still worry if you knew that it was making the situation worse? Worry, after all, is a call for negative results. It affirms the worst-case scenario. If you actually realized the power of your thoughts, you would never choose to worry again. Your desire for a healed outcome is better addressed through surrendering the entire situation to God and us angels. Then ask us for guidance and intervention. Do not tell us how you want the situation healed, for that wisdom is entirely up to God. Please simply trust that your Divine intervention is in process, and a wonderful outcome is being presented to you right now."

Various Meanings of the Card: Focus upon your desires instead of your fears. • Know how powerful you truly are. • Relax; the situation is under control. • Expect a miraculous healing. • Have faith. • Turn the situation over (repeatedly, if necessary) to God and the angels. • Get support from loved ones. • Rest your mind and body.

Suggested Actions to Take After Drawing This Card: Carry a sheet of paper with you and mark an "X" on the paper each time you catch yourself complaining mentally or aloud, then vow to reduce the number of X's each day. • Make a pact with a friend to point out and lovingly correct each other's complaining behavior. • Affirm: *"I am safe, loved, and* *protected,"* and *"It is safe for me to be powerful,"* at least twice a day. • Write down any worries and put them in a "God Box," a special compartment that only you will see; or else put them in the freezer to "freeze" the worries.

ON THE RIGHT PATH

You have chosen wisely. Now keep going!

Message from Your Angels: "Release your worries about your future, and focus instead on moving confidently in this moment, upon the path of light that you have entered. Each moment is illuminated and guided, and you simply need to focus on what you are doing and thinking in each given moment. The rest will take care of itself, we promise. Give any cares and worries to us angels, and we shall cart them away so that your heart, mind, and spirit are lighthearted and filled with energy and great joy!"

Various Meanings of the Card: Stick with your current plan, since it's working. • You're making progress, even if it's not apparent. • The roadblocks you've encountered are temporary and not a sign that you're off the path. • Keep the faith. • You're a lightworker, and the world needs you and your talents. • Your decision is the best one for you and your mission.

Suggested Actions to Take After Drawing This Card: Affirm: "I honor the choices that my inner guidance inspires" at least twice a day. • Ask Archangel Michael to release doubts from your mind and heart. • Reward yourself each time you take steps toward your desires. • Post the word *Faith* in a prominent location where you'll read it often.

ROMANCE ANGELS

The angels are sending you Divine love.

Message from Your Angels: "There is no scarcity of love, for it is all around you, moving through you even now. Your awakening heart greets this love as a new sunrise filled with light, color, and warmth. Notice this love, and your awareness of it shall grow even more. For as you keep your awareness and gaze centered on the magnificence of love, you cannot help but attract its benevolent and miraculous energy into your life. Enjoy this love, and the myriad ways in which it blesses you. Each form of love that enters into a relationship is, in itself, a miracle. And when the love encircles two people who have chosen to spend a lifetime together, we call this romantic love, and yet it is so much more. It is holy indeed."

Various Meanings of the Card: A new partner is entering your life. • Your current partner is your soul mate. • There will be improvements in your relationship. • You'll have renewed passion and fun. • Your heart chakra is opening, and you're feeling more loved and lovable. • A departed lover is thinking of you.

Suggested Actions to Take After Drawing This Card: Notice five or more examples of love today (such as a mother cuddling her child, a helpful person, and so on). • Buy yourself a red rose. • Affirm: *"I am loved, lovable, and loving"* at least three times a day. • Keep your rose quartz crystal in the romance corner of your bedroom to attract romance (this is the southwest, or far right, corner of the room, according to the ancient Chinese art of placement known as *feng shui*). • Pour your heart out in a letter to the guardian angels of your soul mate, asking for help in bringing you together and having a wonderful love relationship.

SELF-APPRECIATION

See the angel within, and love yourself more.

Message from Your Angels: "You are beautiful in all ways, Dear One. Own and know this knowledge deep within your heart. You are a product of the Almighty Creator, and there isn't a hint of damage within or around you. You are perfect! You are the epitome of goodness and light! The more that you see this beauty within yourself, the more you radiate its qualities so that all may benefit. Be a testament to the miracle of life itself. Appreciate and love who you really are, and by so doing, you shall truly know the joys of living. You are a miracle, Beloved One!"

Various Meanings of the Card: Stop self-criticism. • Treat and think of yourself more lovingly. • Release guilt to Heaven. • Take time for yourself and your priorities. • Give yourself permission to pursue your dreams. • Get enough rest, exercise, and healthful nutrition. • Have fun and play more.

Suggested Actions to Take After Drawing This Card: Put your arms around yourself and say, "I love you, self!" • Affirm three or more times as you're falling asleep: *"I am a lovable person."* • Smile and say "Hello" to at least one new person today. • Treat yourself to a special indulgence. • When someone compliments or helps you, simply say "Thank you" without apology.

SUCCESS!

A favorable outcome is assured.

Message from Your Angels: "Do not compare yourself to others when measuring the outcome of your endeavors, for others walk a much different path. Do not seek to gain their compliments or good favor, for such goals will not bring you the happiness you desire. Your success stems from the realization that you are contributing in a way that brings you and others joy. This is the key for which you are seeking. Do not waver from the path of joy, and all of your endeavors will have the mark of success upon them.

Your present situation is ripe to bring you this form of success. Simply stay attuned to your roadmap of joy by keeping your awareness of your inner truth high. It is your feedback system, which will not steer you the wrong way. Stay tuned in to joy, and your success is assured!"

Various Meanings of the Card: Your endeavor will have a favorable outcome. • A healing is imminent. • Allow yourself to succeed. • Your success helps others. • Release fear or guilt to Heaven. • A financial windfall and/or some form of abundance will befall you. • Raise your standards.

Suggested Actions to Take After Drawing This Card: Act, dress, and talk as if your dream is already realized. • Visualize a successful outcome; and notice the accompanying feelings, sounds, and other details of your visualization. • Write a letter to God that begins, "Thank you, God for . . ." and then proceed to write as if all your prayers are already answered. • Donate money, time, or goods to a worthy cause (the ancient practice of tithing always attracts abundance into your life, but don't give with the sole intention of receiving—you must really give and let go for the process to work).

TRUST YOUR INTUITION

Listen to your inner wisdom,
and trust its validity.

Message from Your Angels: "Your inner wisdom is the sage on the high mountain. There is none more wise than your inner self, for it is a reflection of the light and wisdom of Creation. Yet, to reach this state of inner wisdom requires you to quiet your mind and listen without prejudice or agenda. Sit still and breathe. Then notice your thoughts and tell them to be quiet, much as you would calm a crying child. At this point, focus deeply on your inner cache of quiet thoughts, feelings, words, and visions. Do not pay attention to fearful voices, as they are the echoes of the outer world of illusion. Simply notice the truth that your body, heart, and mind speaks to you. Do not judge it, plan around it, or otherwise do anything other than listen to it right now. Once you have heard this wisdom, make a personal pledge to honor it. Only then is it time to take action based upon this sage guidance. This is being true to yourself."

Various Meanings of the Card: Don't second-guess yourself. • Trust the messages you're receiving from your angels. • Pay attention to your feelings. • Balance your tendency to help others by taking good care of yourself. • Avoid situations or relationships with harsh energy. • Stand up for your rights.

Suggested Actions to Take After Drawing This Card: Close your eyes, take a deep breath, and notice how many physical and emotional feelings you can identify within yourself. • Write in your journal about any mixed emotions or confusion as a way to decipher them. • Ask your angels to clarify and amplify their messages to you. • Affirm several times a day: *"I now clearly receive and understand my angels' messages."*

WELCOME THE NEW

This is a change for the better, and new blessings are coming your way.

Message from Your Angels: "Although change can seem intimidating, we assure you that this one ushers in newness as fresh as the morning air. You cannot yet see past indecision and worry to realize the full extent in which this change will ultimately bless you and your loved ones. For this, we ask you to trust. Newness brings some feelings that your world is upside down, and you do not know the order or structure of your day.

Yet, these are the times that allow you to approach life with expanded thinking, creativity, and a renewed appreciation of life and your loved ones. Do not waste time thinking about dark possibilities when so much hope glimmers on the horizon! Know that anything that truly matters—such as love, peace, and understanding—is eternal, and a basis for triumphant stability in the face of change."

Various Meanings of the Card: There will be a major change for the better. • As one door closes, another one's opening for you now. • You'll find a new relationship, or experience an improvement in an existing relationship. • Pay attention to new ideas. • Honor any grief about endings, and know that new blessings are dawning. • Stay flexible and open-minded.

Suggested Actions to Take After Drawing This Card: Clear the energy in your home or workplace through the ancient Chinese art of *feng shui,* burning sage, opening the windows, or calling in the angels. • Notice your breathing frequently throughout the day to ensure that you're taking deep breaths regularly.• Keep up your energy for your life change by eating and exercising extra healthfully right now. • Affirm: *"It is safe for me to make changes in my life."*

YOU ARE SUPPORTED

Allow Heaven to carry you, as well as any burdens you may have.

Message from Your Angels: "At times you feel alone, yet this is impossible in truth. You are connected through love circuits to many profound beings, both on the earth and on spiritual planes. If you insist on carving out a story in which you are unsupported, these love circuits cannot help you. Yet, the moment that you confidently affirm that help surrounds you, your faith is signaled through the love circuit, summoning assistance for you. Move forward confidently, knowing all the while that you *are* supported by those who are rooting for your success, peace, and happiness in all ways. The Universe is working together in your favor, and supports every seeming need you may have for your beautiful life mission and your inner peace."

Various Meanings of the Card: Heaven has heard you and is answering your prayers. • You're being helped by angels on Earth and in Heaven. • Financial support is coming your way. • Your decision is supported by the Universe. • A miraculous intervention helps you. • Allow yourself to receive help and support without guilt or worry.

Suggested Actions to Take After Drawing This Card: Say "Thank you" as a mantra silently, over and over. • Write down any insecurities on a paper; and then burn, bury, or freeze the paper .• Affirm: *"It is safe for me to be helped"* several times a day. • Be extra alert to noticing the gifts that come your way, whether it's a coin on a sidewalk, a helpful person, a friendly letter, or an unexpected windfall.

ARTWORK ORDERING INFORMATION

You can order prints of many of the images from the 12 Angel Oracle Cards. The prints come in various sizes, without the border or words written on the card. To purchase these prints, please contact the artists directly through the methods listed below. Neither Hay House, Inc., Angel Therapy, Inc., nor Doreen Virtue, Ph.D., assumes responsibility for any transactions conducted between you and the individual artists.

Artwork by Audrey L. Arena
Card Names: *No Worries, Romance Angels, Welcome the New, You Are Supported*

Audrey's paintings are realistic fantasy, inspired by Renaissance fairs, her family, pets, and the Bible. Her favorite artistic theme is "Scenes of the Peaceful Kingdom"; and her paintings of exotic scenery, animals, and people in their costumes in the settings they dream of, reflect this. Audrey attends Harley-Davidson events and paints on motorcycles, canvas, collector eggs, and more.
Contact info: *Website:* **www.fantasyartbyaudrey.com**

Artwork by Sue Halstenberg
Card Names: *Success!, Trust Your Intuition*

Sue began her artistic career in 1979 as a fashion illustrator. Winning numerous awards for her fine art, she earned a Signature Membership from the Pastel Society of America, and her pastel "Victoria" was featured on the cover of *American Artist Magazine.* After communicating with her angels in 1992, Sue started producing healing images from the nonphysical world, revealing more of the true self within. This unique ability to join natural beauty and feminine ideals is expressed through her subjects of angels, fairies, mermaids, and goddesses.

Sue paints and teaches at her hillside studio in California with inspiring views of the beautiful Ojai Valley. She holds a BFA degree from the prestigious Art Center College of Design in Pasadena.

Contact info: *Mailing address:* P.O. Box 356, Ojai, CA 93024 • *Website:* **www.suehalstenberg.com**

Artwork by Lisa Iris
Card Name: *Self-Appreciation*

Lisa's artwork is known worldwide. She says, "My dream is to show people the treasure in their own lives." She's a member of Transcend: Art and Peace Network (**www.tapnet.info**).

Contact info: *Website:* **www.lisairis.com** (for artwork) or **www.whitewolfgallery.bigstep.com** (for jewelry and prints of Lisa's art).

Artwork by Elizabeth Kyle
Card Name: *Gratitude*

Born in New Zealand, Elizabeth now lives in the picturesque Currumbin Valley, Gold Coast, Australia. A professional artist for 33 years, she brings the best of the past to the present with her Celtic-inspired depictions of our Soul's Journey. She is also known in New Zealand by her maiden name, Elizabeth Grainger, for her "New Zealand paintings" (1972–83). Elizabeth is internationally acclaimed for her Visionary Surrealist artworks, which emanate from lucid visions, inspired by her love of Mother Earth. Her paintings are like parables, with personal as well as global messages. She has held sold-out exhibitions and won many national awards.

Her art has graced book and magazine covers, as well as greeting cards.

Contact info: *Mailing address:* P.O. Box 609, Currumbin Valley, 4223 QLD, Australia • *Website:* **www.elizabethkyle.com** • *e-mail:* ekyle@optusnet.com.au

Artwork by September McGee
Card Name: *Golden Opportunity*

September is an artist and author whose inspirational works are found in collections all over the world. Most recently, her artwork was shown at the White House.

Contact info: *Website:* **www.septembermcgee.com** • *Phone:* (949) 499-0274

Artwork by Shirley Morales
Card Names: *Family, On the Right Path*

Shirley Mischael-Morales's watercolor paintings of angels and fairies are inspired by a desire to share the joy of the nurturing presence and ever-available protective guidance of the unseen realms. Shirley teaches yoga and meditation and leads art explorations groups for children and teens. She is also a certified Angel Therapy Practitioner who gives angel and mediumship readings and healings, and she personally trained with Doreen Virtue. She shares her time between her home in Oregon's scenic Columbia River Gorge and California.

Contact info: Emerald Visions & White Meadow • *Mailing address:* P.O. Box 180 Corbett, OR 97019 • *Website:* **www.Emeraldvisionsart.com** • *e-mail:* contact@emeraldvisionsart.com • *Phone:* (503) 695-2175 or toll-free: (877) 659-2319

Artwork by Monica Tibbetts
Card Name: *Ask Your Angels*

Monica lives in Moab, Utah. She's been painting for 25 years. Her artwork includes oil, acrylic, and watercolor pictures and portraits. Angels have always helped her, and she feels that it's her calling to portray them in "Angel Art" so people will remember to connect with their higher source daily.

Contact info: *e-mail:* MonicaCountess@hotmail.com • *Mailing address:* P.O. Box 891 Moab, UT 84532

ABOUT THE AUTHOR

Doreen Virtue, Ph.D., holds three university degrees in counseling psychology. She's a clairvoyant fourth-generation metaphysician who works with the angelic, elemental, and ascended-master realms in her writing and workshops. Her books and oracle cards include *Messages from Your Angels, Archangels & Ascended Masters, Magical Mermaids and Dolphins, Healing with the Fairies,* and *Healing with the Angels* (all published by Hay House). She's also the author of many books and audio programs relating to angels, psychic development, and mind/body/spirit topics.

Doreen frequently appears on television and radio, where she's known as "The Angel Lady." For more information on Doreen's workshops, books, tapes, and cards; to subscribe to her free e-mail newsletter; or to participate in her online community message board, please visit her Website at: **www.AngelTherapy.com**. For a catalog of Doreen's products, please contact Hay House.

We hope you enjoyed this Hay House Lifestyles guidebook. If you would like to receive a free catalog featuring additional Hay House books and products, or if you would like information about the Hay Foundation, please contact:

Hay House, Inc.
P.O. Box 5100
Carlsbad, CA 92018-5100

(760) 431-7695 or **(800) 654-5126**
(760) 431-6948 (fax) or **(800) 650-5115 (fax)**
www.hayhouse.com

Published and distributed in Australia by:
Hay House Australia Pty. Ltd. • 18/36 Ralph St. • Alexandria NSW 2015 • *Phone:* 612-9669-4299 • *Fax:* 612-9669-4144
www.hayhouse.com.au

Published and distributed in the United Kingdom by:
Hay House UK, Ltd. • Unit 62, Canalot Studios • 222 Kensal Rd., London W10 5BN • *Phone:* 44-20-8962-1230
Fax: 44-20-8962-1239 • www.hayhouse.co.uk

Published and distributed in the Republic of South Africa by:
Hay House SA (Pty), Ltd., P.O. Box 990, Witkoppen 2068
Phone/Fax: 2711-7012233 • orders@psdprom.co.za

Distributed in Canada by:
Raincoast • 9050 Shaughnessy St., Vancouver, B.C. V6P 6E5
Phone: (604) 323-7100 • *Fax:* (604) 323-2600

Sign up via the Hay House USA Website to receive the Hay House online newsletter and stay informed about what's going on with your favorite authors. You'll receive bimonthly announcements about: Discounts and Offers, Special Events, Product Highlights, Free Excerpts, Giveaways, and more!
www.hayhouse.com